The
Funniest Moments
in Sports

Herman L. Masin

THE

FUNNIEST MOMENTS

IN SPORTS

Illustrated by Kevin Callahan

M. Evans and Company, Inc.

New York, N.Y. 10017

To three terrific sportsmen who never dreamed
they'd have a book dedicated to them:
Wayne Terwilliger, Bevo Francis, and
Bob Clatterbuck

CATCHES IN THE WRY
★ Baseball ★

INDIAN GIVER

The manager sought out his second baseman.

"Billy," he said, "remember all those batting tips, double-play pivots, and base-running hints I gave you this afternoon?"

"Sure, Skipper."

"Forget 'em! We've just traded you to Kansas City."

LONG DISTANCE

With Dick Allen at bat, the pitcher kept shaking off the catcher. Finally the catcher walked out to the mound.

"You're gonna have to throw him something. So, come on, pitch the ball."

"Let's wait a while," begged the pitcher. "Maybe he'll get a long-distance phone call."

ACE HIGH

When Johnny Mize played first base for the Giants, he wouldn't or couldn't bend down to field a ball. In fact he seldom went after anything that wasn't hit straight back at him.

This moved humorist Goodman Ace to wire manager Leo Durocher:

"Sir: Before each game an announcement is made that anyone interfering with or touching a batted ball will be ejected from the park. Please advise Mr. Mize that this doesn't apply to him."

HANDS OFF

Most old-time catchers have hands like weather vanes, with fingers pointing in different directions.

"When two old catchers meet on the street and shake hands," claims Joe Garagiola, "it takes a plumber twenty minutes to pry them apart."

The Kansas City Athletics once had several knuckle-ball pitchers. So they had to stock several oversized catcher's mitts. Coach Mel McGaha kept one of them in his room. One day the maid saw it in the closet and asked McGaha what it was.

"Oh, we use that to catch knuckle balls," he explained.

"Gee," replied the maid, "are knuckle balls that big?"

MOVING DAY

Live wire Johnny Bench noticed a teammate goofing off during infield practice.

"Hey, man, get with it!" he yelled. "You've been standing around so long, they're going to make a ground rule out of you!"

BLOW HARD

Ron Swoboda came into the clubhouse after fanning five times.

"I ought to get my .38 and blow my head off," he moaned.

"Don't bother," grunted a coach. "With your eye you would probably miss."

BROCK-BUSTER

Lou Brock robbed the Pirates with a fantastic catch. Pirate manager Bill Virdon shook his head.

"I don't believe it," he said. "Brock could never make that play again—not even on instant replay."

DEM GOLDEN SLIPPERS

Henry Aaron was asked to comment about Pete Rose's hustle.

"Does Pete hustle? Before the All-Star Game he came into the clubhouse and took off his shoes—and they ran another mile without him."

MAKE-BELIEVE

Frank Howard has always been a great slugger. But no one has ever accused him of being able to catch a fly ball. One winter he heard that some big fellow was making the rounds of nightclubs, stores, etc., impersonating him. Howard hit on a plan for catching the rascal.

"Next time anyone comes around claiming he's Frank Howard," he suggested, "take him outside and fungo a fly ball to him. If he catches it, call the cops."

RUNS FOR YOUR LIFE

The sports editor of a Montreal newspaper received a phone call from a wild Expo fan.

"How many runs did the Expos make today?" asked the fan.

"Nineteen."

"Did they win or lose?"

BLOWING TAPS

Amos Otis was at bat one night and didn't like how the umpire was calling 'em. When the man in blue called "Strike three!" Otis blew his top.

"Listen, ump," he snapped, "how can you sleep with the lights on?"

ONLY IN AMERICA

When Robert Briscoe, mayor of Dublin, visited the United States, Yogi Berra was told that Briscoe was the first Jewish mayor in Dublin's history.

"Isn't that great!" Yogi exclaimed. "It could happen only in America."

Vida Blue can throw just about as fast as anyone. One day Thurman Munson stepped in against him, and it was *buzz-buzz-buzz*—three quick strikes. The Yankee catcher walked back to the dugout, put his bat into the rack, and sat down.

"He threw me the radio ball," he said.

"Radio ball?" asked teammate Bobby Murcer.

"That's right. You can hear it but you can't see it."

OUT OF TOUCH

Some years ago Joe Pepitone hit what appeared to be a game-winning home run. The Yankee fans went wild, then groaned as the umpire called Pepitone out for failing to touch second.

Manager Ralph Houk rushed out to argue the call. On the way he passed his first-base coach.

"Don't argue too long, Ralph," the coach advised. "He missed first, too."

PEOPLE IN GLASS HOUSES

After suffering from headaches for a month, the umpire went to a doctor. The doctor gave him a checkup and told him, "There's nothing seriously wrong. I think you need glasses."

The ump bounced up from his chair, jerked his thumb in the air, and roared, "That will cost you a hundred bucks and what's more you're outta the game!"

NO CATCH

The Braves' manager decided to start a rookie pitcher. The first Cardinal hitter laced the first pitch into center for a single. The next batter hit the right-field wall for a double. The third hitter put the first pitch over the wall. The Cardinals then collected a triple, a double, and another triple—each on the first pitch.

The manager walked to the mound. Then he called the catcher over and asked, "What kind of pitch is he throwin', anyway?"

"I don't know," the catcher replied, "I haven't caught any yet."

WHAT A RELIEF

Sparky Lyle bailed out Fritz Peterson a dozen times during the 1972 season. When they went on a joint speaking tour after the season, one of the team wits put it this way, "I hear that Peterson will speak for seven minutes and then Sparky will take over for the last two minutes."

TIME MARCHES ON

The White Sox brought up an 18-year-old rookie from a little town in Arkansas. Manager Chuck Tanner placed the kid next to him on the bench so that he could teach him some of the finer points of the game.

In the second inning, Mike Andrews drew a base on balls. The next batter lined a hit down the right-field line.

Andrews correctly wheeled around second and went to third—only to be cut down by a fantastic throw.

Turner turned to the rookie and said, "Andrews was right to try for third. You won't see another throw like that in a hundred years."

In the seventh inning with Andrews again on first, the same batter lined to the same spot and the same outfielder made the same kind of throw to nail Andrews trying for third!

The rookie on the bench tapped Tanner on the shoulder and said, "Mistuh Tanner, time sure flies fast heah in the No'th."

HEAR, HEAR!

The center-field wall in Cincinnati's Crosley Field had a yellow line that divided the top wooden section from the bottom concrete area. Any drive above the line was considered a home run.

One afternoon, with the bags full of Mets, Ron Swoboda drove one close to the yellow line. The ball bounced back to the center fielder, and umpire Frank Secory signaled the ball in play. Swoboda wound up with just a single.

The Mets stormed at the ump. They argued that while it was hard to *see* whether the ball had hit above or below the yellow line, the *sound* should have tipped off the umpire. A ball striking concrete made a clicking noise, while a ball striking wood made a boom sound—and this had been a boom.

Yogi Berra, then the Mets' coach, put in the final word:

"What's the matter with you, Secory? Anybody who can't hear the difference must be blind."

Dick Stuart, the wandering first baseman, never won a Golden Glove for his fielding, but the fans loved him all the same. One day a bat slipped from the hitter's hands and bounced all the way to first base. Stuart fielded it cleanly and the crowd went wild cheering him.

After the game, the big first baseman was asked if that had been the biggest hand he had ever received.

"Heck, no," he replied. "One night in Pittsburgh 30,000 fans gave me a standing ovation when I caught a hot-dog wrapper on the fly."

A FINE DAY

It was steaming in Houston, and the wilted Cubs lost three in a row in the Astrodome. The Cubs' manager got so tired of hearing his players bellyache about the heat, he threatened a 50-buck fine the next time he caught anyone mentioning the temperature.

Glenn Beckert staggered to the bench after a run-down. He mopped the sweat from his brow and muttered, "Man, it's steaming out there."

Then, catching his manager frowning at him, he quickly added, "But *nice*."

ON THE FENCE

Reggie Smith doesn't believe in banging into fences going after long flies. When a pitcher bugs him about it, Reggie replies, "Why should I go jackknifing over the fence on my head? That ball has got no business being out there 400 feet."

MADE IN JAPAN

The Dodgers were shut out three times in a row in the 1966 World Series. They then flew to Japan on a goodwill tour and won the first game, 5-3. The wire report to the United States that day read:

"The Dodgers are the first team in history that had to leave the country to score a run."

SNAKE IN THE GRASS

In his early years with the Mets, Casey Stengel didn't have a catcher who could handle low pitches. As he explained to the press, "What we need behind the bat is a snake with a mitt."

WINNING TICKET

Denny McLain came into New York on August 22, 1968, looking for his 26th win of the season. A reporter cornered him.

"Tell me, Denny, what do you think of more—winning the pennant or winning 30 games?"

"That's easy to answer," replied Denny. "Winning the pennant is everything. I don't even think of winning 30—except every minute of the day."

THE BIG SLEEP

The umpire grew tired of the riding he was taking from the home team. He called time and strode to the dugout. By the time he got there, the players had lapsed into silence. They lay slumped in all directions, snoring and wheezing as if asleep.

The umpire shook his head. "OK, sleep if you want to. But if one of you wakes up before the game is over, I'm going to fine him a hundred bucks!"

WHERE THERE'S A WILL

A fast ball caught the batter on the knee and he fell to the ground in agony. Out rushed the trainer, who began to vigorously rub the knee.

"How does the knee feel now?" asked the trainer.

"Great."

"I thought so," replied the trainer. "It doesn't look swollen and it feels pretty firm."

"Doc," groaned the player, "you've been rubbing the wrong knee."

PLATE BREAKER

Mel Stottlemyre broke his famous curve ball over the corner, and umpire Lou Di Muro called it a strike. The batter gave him a dirty look.

"Where was that pitch?" he demanded.

"Right over the outside corner," snapped the ump.

The batter looked at him coldly. "I don't see any corner on the plate where that ball crossed."

Di Muro looked down as if to inspect the plate.

"You're right," he said. "That curve was so sharp it clipped the corner right off."

PLENTY OF NUTHIN'

Good umpires always make it clear who is boss. In a close play at home one afternoon, umpire Shag Crawford hesitated on the call.

"Well, is he safe or out?" barked the catcher.

"Son," remarked Crawford softly, "until I call it, it's nuthin'."

DEATHLESS ERROR

One day a well-known local doctor was making life miserable for the third-base umpire. The ump took it as long as he could. Finally he stopped the game and marched over to the stands. Pointing a finger at the doctor, he roared:

"You got no right to beef, Doc. When you make a mistake, it's followed by a funeral. When I make a mistake, it lives forever!"

INTERNATIONAL ANTHEM

An Irishman named O'Shea came to America and wanted to see a big league game. Since the game was a sellout, the management set him up on the flagpole.

When O'Shea returned to Ireland, his neighbors asked him, "What kind of people are the Americans?"

"Great!" he said. "They gave me a special seat and just before the game started, they all stood up and sang, 'O'Shea can you see.' "

RED, RED ROBIN

One of Robin Roberts's most notable feats was fanning three Pirates in a row after being hit for a triple. He whiffed Pete Castiglione on five pitches, Ralph Kiner on four, and Joe Garagiola on just three. This made Garagiola mad.

"It's embarrassing," he complained. "He should have at least *worked* on me."

MONEY-BACK GUARANTEE

The Cardinals signed their No. 1 draft choice for $100,000. He was supposed to be a greater switch-hitter than Mickey Mantle. Manager Red Schoendienst soon found out that the big bonus baby had a hitch in his swing. He called the rookie to his office and asked, "Do you have a hitch in your swing?"

"Yes, sir, I guess I do."

"Which way—righty or lefty?"

"Only lefty," the rookie replied. "I'm OK righty."

"Fine," said Schoendienst. "Then you only have to give us back $50,000."

THINK A DRINK

Umpire Ed Vargo was once taking a needling from a big crowd. He suffered in silence, until a husky female fan in a box seat behind him shouted:

"If I were your wife, I'd give you poison!"

Vargo removed his mask and turned around. He bowed to the lady and replied in a loud, clear voice:

"And if I were your husband, madam, I'd take it."

SOUND OF MU-ZZZ-IC

After a week of rooming with the rookie third-baseman, the veteran shortstop demanded another room. He claimed that something had to be done about the rookie's snoring.

"Aw, c'mon," his manager said, "you can take a little snoring."

"It's not his snoring so much," explained the shortstop. "I could stand that. But the tugboats out in the bay have started answering him."

Joe Pepitone took a long lead off first, then went into a trance. A snap throw from the catcher awakened him. Desperately he dove back to the bag. Before the umpire could make his call, Pepitone began screaming, "I made it! I made it!"

"Sure you did, Joe," said the ump, jerking his thumb to the sky. "But what took you so long?"

SWEET BIRD OF YOUTH

Joe DiMaggio was telling how a player learns that his youth is going.

"You start chasing a ball and your brain immediately commands your body to 'Run forward! Bend! Scoop up the ball! Peg it to the infield!'"

"Then what happens?" asked a friend.

"Then," Joe said, "your body says, 'Who, me?'"

LOVE AND MARRIAGE

With the opening day of baseball season just 24 hours away, the office boy asked for a day off.

"What is it this time?" snapped the office manager. "You've asked time off for your grandfather's funeral four times already."

"Today," replied the boy, "my grandmother is getting married again."

The rookie Cub pitcher couldn't get anyone out. The hitters were whistling line drives in all directions, and several of the infielders became fearful of their lives.

Ron Santo, the third baseman, strolled over to the pitcher.

"Can't you walk a few of these guys?" he begged, feeling the lumps on his shins.

The rookie wiped the sweat from his brow.

"Get back there, you coward," he snapped. "I'm a lot closer to them than you are."

DOUBLE TROUBLE

One day the Cincinnati pitcher fanned Billy Williams on a pitch that escaped the catcher, letting Williams dash all the way to second. Red manager Sparky Anderson heaved a sigh.

"That guy Billy Williams is so good," he said, "that even when he fans, a team is lucky to hold him to two bases."

INSTANT OLD AGE

A 12-year-old boy approached Danny Ozark for a tryout. The Philadelphia manager told him to come back in a few years.

Two days later the boy showed up again.

"I told you, sonny," said Ozark, "to come back when you're older."

"Mr. Ozark," replied the boy, "I watched your Phillies play the Dodgers yesterday. That aged me ten years."

HEADACHE

Casey Stengel was trying to teach Ron Hunt how to pull the ball to left.

"Look, kid," he said, "watch me do it." He took Hunt's bat and stepped into the box. The pitcher uncorked a wild pitch that conked Stengel on the head. The old man went down like a light. He rolled around in the dust for a while, then slowly rose to his feet.

"Forget about the lesson for today," he told Hunt. "That big ape just put me on base."

THE NO-NOTHING

Bo Belinsky was getting his lumps. By the seventh inning, the Tigers had a 15-0 lead. Bo came back to the dugout looking disgusted.

"What's eating you, Bo?" asked a teammate.

"What do you think?" replied Belinsky. "How can a guy win a game if you don't give him any runs?"

GRIMM STORY

Win or lose, old Cub manager Charlie Grimm never lost his poise or sense of humor. One afternoon, after the Cubs had dropped their 14th game in a row, Charlie walked into the press room. Before he could be asked a question, he raised his hand.

"Gentlemen," he said, "you can't win them all."

LETTER PERFECT

In his first season with the Yankees, Lefty Gomez begged manager Joe McCarthy for a chance to start a game. Finally Joe agreed. As luck would have it, Gomez was bombed.

After the game, McCarthy took Gomez aside and told him that he was giving him his release.

"Well, I can't blame you," said Gomez, "but would you mind giving me a letter of recommendation?"

"Sure," answered the manager and wrote the following letter: "Lefty Gomez pitched one game for me and I am satisfied."

BAD BOUNCE

Steve Carlton was laboring on the mound. His infielders kept booting one ground ball after the other, but the big lefty never complained. He merely nodded whenever a fielder apologized after a boot, "Bad bounce, Steve. Sorry."

The ninth inning found the score 4-4, an opponent on third and two out. The batter lifted a towering pop fly that the shortstop circled under, reached for—and dropped. The runner on third scored and Carlton lost the game.

As the shortstop plodded into the dugout, Carlton beat him to the punch, "Bad bounces up there, too, you bum?"

George Moriarty was umpiring a Cleveland-Detroit game. An Indian rookie was up at the plate. The rookie took one strike without protest. He took another. And then a third. Before returning to the dugout, he turned to the umpire.

"I beg your pardon," he politely said, "but how do you spell your name?"

Surprised, Moriarty spelled out his name letter by letter. The rookie nodded.

"Just as I thought, sir, only one *i*."

HOOK, LINE, AND SINKER

Jay Hook was one of the few mental giants to play in the big leagues. He had an I.Q. of around 150 plus several college degrees. He also had good "stuff" as a pitcher. But somehow he never made it big. Some of the players thought he was just too smart to be an outstanding pitcher.

"He should forget about those big words," remarked one of his teammates. "You can't get them out in the library."

GROOM FOR TWO

The Pirates once had a pair of outfielders who were so handsome they could have been actors. Both of them were very aware of their good looks.

One afternoon Joe Garagiola walked into the dressing

room and found them grooming themselves in front of the mirror. Garagiola watched them silently for a moment, then cracked:

"If you two guys ever lost your combs, they'd have to call off the game."

SITTING PRETTY

When Paul Popovich was with the Cubs, he seldom saw any action. Glenn Beckert played second base every day.

One day the Cubs were losing by a lopsided score and manager Leo Durocher decided to rest Beckert. He told Popovich to warm up, then asked one of his coaches what the score was.

"It's 9-2," he was told.

"Sit down, Paul," ordered Durocher. "We ain't giving up yet."

CHANGE OF SPACE

Jerry Koosman was having trouble getting the Giants out. Willie McCovey whacked two long homers off him. After the second clout, manager Gil Hodges yanked Koosman, who started for the showers. Hodges called him back.

"Sit right here," he said. "I want you to see how Tug McGraw pitches to McCovey."

When Willie came up again, McGraw turned on the power. *Crash!* This time Willie parked one in the left-field stands. A silence followed. Then Koosman nodded.

"I see," he said. "Tug made him change direction."

THE MAIL ANIMAL

After winning the World Series in 1963, the Dodgers took a deep dive in 1964. One of the worst slumpers was relief pitcher Ron Perranoski. Naturally this had an effect on his fan mail. In the clubhouse one evening, Perranoski quipped to a nearby coach:

"To show you what kind of a year I'm having, all I found in my mailbox was a moth—and it snapped at me."

AN OLD GROUCHO

The Giants started the 1951 season with 11 straight defeats. The following Sunday Tallulah Bankhead, a Giant fan, had Groucho Marx on her radio show.

"Don't worry about the Giants," she told him. "Remember, Leo Durocher is leading them."

"Yes," snapped Groucho, "and so is everyone else in the league."

BLIND RAGE

The umpire called an Expo out at the plate, and the fans went wild. Several players made a dash for the umpire, and manager Gene Mauch leaped out of the dugout. Laying a hand on the ump's head, Mauch glared at his players and roared:

"The first guy who lays a finger on this blind old man is fined fifty bucks!"

SAY UNCLE

An office boy was at a ball game when his boss suddenly came up behind him.

"So this is your uncle's funeral, eh?" he snapped.

"Looks like it," the boy replied. "He's the umpire down there."

SALT OF THE EARTH

Charley Gehringer was probably the quietest ball player who ever lived. But in Chief Hogsett, his Tiger roomie, Gehringer found a blood brother.

In all the years they roomed together, the players had only one argument. It happened over breakfast one morning when Hogsett leaned across the table and said, "Charley, please pass the salt."

Gehringer stiffened. He made no effort to oblige. The meal continued in silence. Finally, Hogsett asked, "Did I say anything wrong, Charley?"

"You could have pointed," Gehringer replied.

DEVILISH IDEA

The big league manager dreamed he was in heaven. Everywhere he looked he saw a Hall of Fame player. So he formed a team. The phone rang. It was the devil.

"I have a team that can beat yours," said Satan.

"Impossible!" bellowed the manager. "I've got the greatest players of all time."

"Yeah," replied the devil, "but I've got all the umpires."

BLAST-OFF

It happened during a Little League World Series game. The catcher asked for time out to clean his mask.

"What happened?" the umpire asked.

"My bubble gum exploded!" chirped the boy.

"SAFE" CRACKING

Ralph Houk was telling umpire Bill Haller it was a cinch to umpire. "All you have to do is jerk your right arm up and roar, 'Yer-r-r ow-w-wit!' I could do that all day."

"No, you couldn't," said the umpire. "Supposing the runner was safe?"

WHAT'S IN A NAME

Called out at second base, Jimmy Wynn let off some steam. The umpire promptly heaved him out of the game. That brought his manager, Harry Walker, onto the field.

"Why'd you throw him out of the game?" Walker demanded.

"Because he said I was blind and stupid and he called me a dirty name," snarled the ump.

"Leave off the dirty name," replied Walker, "and how wrong was he?"

TAKE A WALK

The first time up Houston's Cesar Cedeno tripled. The second time he put one over the wall. Then he slugged a pair of doubles. Next time up he walked on a three-and-two count.

The call made Cub catcher Randy Hundley unhappy. He turned to the ump and growled, "You sure put him on base that time."

"Maybe I did," agreed the ump. "But at least I held him to one base."

BEHIND EVERY MAN

It is agreed that Dick Stuart was the worst-fielding first baseman of modern times. He was nicknamed "Dr. Strangeglove."

"Believe me," he once told a writer, "getting married was the greatest thing that ever happened to me. It straightened me out. Behind every successful man stands a good woman."

"With a first baseman's mitt?" asked the writer.

Hank Aaron was taking batting practice. He belted the first ball 400 feet into the left center stands, where a fan made a fine bare-handed catch.

A moment later Henry belted another ball into the same sector, where the same fan made another great stab—and got a tremendous cheer.

Aaron grinned. "That guy is sure playing me right."

CALLING ALL ELEPHANTS

Umpire Ed Runge was needling Boog Powell about his .220 batting average. "Boy, you're a miserable hitter these days. Why, if somebody threw you an *elephant*, you couldn't hit it."

"Ed," Powell said, "if somebody threw me an elephant, you couldn't *call* it."

FEUD FOR THOUGHT

Back in his Dodger days, Jackie Robinson had a bitter feud with sportswriter Mike Gaven. One night when Gaven entered the dugout, Jackie took out after him.

"You writers are always wrong, always wrong," he yelped.

Gaven looked him up and down, then softly replied, "You mean like when we voted you Most Valuable Player last year?"

SPRINT TIME

Yankee pitching coach Jim Turner liked to run his charges' legs off. One afternoon he noticed pitcher Steve Kline leaning against the centerfield fence, panting like a marathon runner.

"What's the matter?" Turner drawled. "Feeling a bit tired? You know you gotta keep running if you want to have a big year."

"Heck," moaned Kline, "if running was so important, Jim Ryun would be a 20-game winner."

AMONG THE MISSING

The Tiger pitcher got blasted for six hits and seven runs in three innings.

"It's this way," he explained to manager Billy Martin. "My fast ball doesn't have that little something extra—and when that little something extra is missing, a lot of baseballs are sure to follow."

RUBBER DUB-DUB

The American League was thinking of changing the size of the pitching rubber. They asked the advice of its greatest pitcher, Bob Feller.

"It makes no difference to me," shrugged Feller.

"But it should," insisted a club president. "After all, your livelihood depends upon where you stand on the rubber."

"Nonsense," retorted Feller. "I never fooled anyone with my feet."

34

WILLING SPIRIT

The baseball coach was selling tickets for a benefit game. He approached the town banker and asked how many tickets he would like.

"I'm sorry. I won't be able to make it," was the answer. "But I want you to know my spirit will be there with you."

"Good," snapped the coach. "I have a fine selection of one, two, and three dollar seats. Where would your spirit like to sit?"

DOG-GONE IT

The game was going into extra innings and the two rooters didn't want to march back to the refreshment stand. They snagged a nearby kid.

"Hey, kid, here's a-buck-twenty. Get us two franks and buy one for yourself."

The kid returned ten minutes later with 80 cents change.

"Sorry," he explained, "they only had *my* hot dog left."

CALL OF THE WILD

Yogi Berra was famous for swinging at bad pitches. One day he went fishing for a terrible pitch—very high and outside—and struck out. A deep silence greeted him in the dugout. Yogi waited vainly for a word from someone. Finally he blurted:

"How can a pitcher that wild stay in the league?"

Every now and then a team tries to change its nickname. It seldom works. The Boston Braves never could get anyone to call them the Bees, and the Phillies had no better luck trying to switch to the Blue Jays.

Even the Daughters of the American Revolution failed to force the Cincinnati Reds to become the Redlegs. (The D.A.R. thought that "Reds" sounded too communistic.)

"Let the Russians change their name," wrote a fan. "We were the Reds before they were."

WORKING OVERTIME

In a late-spring exhibition game, the Dodgers belted Tom Seaver all over the lot in the first inning. Coach Rube Walker was sent to the mound to yank him.

"It's only a practice game," Seaver protested. "Let me stay in. I need the work."

"Sure you do," grinned third baseman Jim Fregosi, "but the outfielders are getting more than they can use."

TIGER RAG

Burly Johnny Blatnik tried to score from second base on a blooper to left field. The small but sturdy catcher, Tiger Tappe, blocked the plate. As the ball spanked into his mitt, Blatnik pounded into him. Tappe was sent crashing into the backstop. He lay there quivering as the umpire rushed up to him.

36

"Tappe," the umpire bellowed, "if you got that ball, that guy is out!"

"Got that ball?" groaned the catcher. "I haven't even got my shinguards!"

LONG INNING

The manager came out to the mound, but the pitcher refused to leave the game.

"Gee, I can handle the next hitter," he insisted. "I struck him out the first time I faced him, remember?"

"Yeah," the manager agreed sadly, "but that was *this* inning."

WALK IN THE SUN

The reporter ran into an old-timer who began bragging about what a great hitter he had been.

"My lifetime batting average was .390, and I wouldda hit .800 if them pitchers weren't afraid to pitch to me."

As the two men reached a corner, the traffic light changed and the W*alk* sign lit up.

"See," the old-timer chuckled, "they're still afraid to pitch to me!"

DOWN AND OUT

Umpire Jack Guthrie made an art of throwing a player

out of a game. One afternoon a batter, angered at a third strike, hurled his bat high into the air. Guthrie cocked his head to follow it.

"If that bat comes down," he drawled, "you're out of the game."

STICK WORK

Sandy Koufax was one of the worst hitters in history. One day he took a mighty swing and, to everyone's amazement, drove a triple to deep center.

Perched on third, Sandy whispered to Coach Billy Herman, "Billy, I think I can steal home."

Herman groaned, "Sandy, it's taken you five years to get this far. Hang around a while and enjoy it."

24-HOUR RECALL

Many old-timers claim that Josh Gibson was the greatest catcher of all time. And they could be right. One thing is sure: the fabulous black catcher could hit a ball out of sight.

That's exactly what he did one hazy afternoon in the Pittsburgh ball park. The umpire waited a long while for the ball to come down. When it didn't, he had to rule it a home run.

In Philadelphia the next day, as Gibson stepped into the batter's box, a ball suddenly zoomed out of space and was caught by the center fielder.

"Yer out!" shouted the umpire. "I mean yesterday, in Pittsburgh!"

FOR A CHANGE

Experts believe that if Nolan Ryan ever developed a change of pace to go with his fast ball, there'd be no other pitcher like him.

"They used to say the same thing about me," claims Hall of Fame pitcher Lefty Gomez. "My manager spent ten years trying to teach me a change of pace. At the end of my career that's all I had left—and there was no other pitcher like me."

SATCHEL PRAISE

In Babe Ruth's first year with the Yankees, he roomed with Ping Bodie. But they were roomies only in name. The Babe was such a night owl that Bodie never saw him.

Someone once asked Bodie, "Who are you rooming with?"

"Babe Ruth's valises," he replied.

FANNING BEE

The nice old lady was watching her first game. She saw Bob Gibson strike out thirteen Giants and allow just one hit. She left the park unhappy. Her only comment was:

"It's a good thing the Giants got that hit. Otherwise we wouldn't have seen *anything*!"

Marv Throneberry was having a tough time at first base. He fumbled four ground balls and manager Casey Stengel finally had to bench him. That evening Marvelous Marv was sitting in the hotel lobby, looking sad, when Stengel walked by.

"What's the matter, Marv?" asked the manager.

"Today's my birthday," Marv replied, "and nobody gave me a cake."

Stengel shook his head sadly. "Marv," he said, "if I thought you could hold on to it, I'd give you one."

Don Newcombe was one of those pitchers who always complained about something—real or fancied. One year he kept insisting that his arm hurt.

"It's all in your imagination," manager Burt Shotton told him.

A day or two later Shotton told Newcombe to start warming up. Big Newk took a couple of pitches and winced with pain.

"My imagination is hurting again," he told Shotton.

PADDLE BALL

With two out and a runner on second in the 12th inning, Don Hoak of the Cubs nubbed one down the first-base line. Gil Hodges swooped down, but the ball hit the bag and spun toward second. Hodges made a stab for it, but the ball twisted away. He stabbed again, and again.

Then Jackie Robinson horned in and the Dodger pair began flailing away as if trying to nail a rattler with canoe paddles.

Finally Hodges looked up. Hoak was safe at first and the winning run was crossing the plate.

"Hit it again, Jackie," he called. "It's still breathing."

BOMBS AWAY!

Mickey Mantle came into the 1961 World Series weak,

beat, and crippled. All eyes were on him when he stepped up for batting practice the first day in Cincinnati.

Batting right-handed against practice-pitcher Spud Murphy, Mantle clouted the first four serves over the left-field fence, the fifth against the fence, and the sixth and seventh pitches against the scoreboard.

Mickey made no effort to conceal his glee.

"Come on, Spud!" he yelled. "Give me something good to swing at!"

TWO FOR THE MONEY

"How many players would it take to make the Texas Rangers a pennant winner?" manager Whitey Herzog was asked.

"Two," was the answer.

"Only two? You must be kidding."

"No, sir," smiled Herzog. "Just Babe Ruth and Sandy Koufax."

SAY WHEN

The Braves were trailing the old Dodgers 5-2 in the bottom of the ninth. The bases were loaded with two out. The batter lined one straight at Babe Herman in right field.

The Great Screwball started in, stopped, and tried to go back, only to slip on the grass. He scrambled to his feet, chased the ball to the fence, tried to pick it up. He fumbled it twice. He then kicked it around a little.

42

He finally found the handle and threw the ball toward the plate—right over the backstop. All the runners scored, and a sure Dodger victory had suddenly turned into a defeat.

As the shocked players trudged to the clubhouse, the Dodger manager went over to Herman.

"What happened, Babe?" he asked.

The Great **Screwball** thought for a moment.

"When?" he said.

HEAVENLY TRIBUTE

Rusty Staub stood behind the batting cage, watching manager Yogi Berra pitch batting practice.

"If I could bat against that kind of pitching all season, I'd be a better hitter," he remarked.

Tom Seaver snorted. "If you ever got to be a better hitter," he said, "they'd name a church after you."

The veteran catcher walked out on the mound to discuss signals with the rookie pitcher.

"Well, son, what kind of pitches do you have?"

"I've got a fast ball, a slow ball, a great screwball, four different kinds of curves, a drop, two kinds of. . . ."

"Whoa, there!" interrupted the catcher. "I have a glove on one hand and only five fingers on the other. How can I signal for so many pitches?"

"Well," snapped the rookie, "take off your shoes and use your toes."

PIGGY BANK

The two teams were playing on an open field. The batter hit one over the outfielders' heads. Before a fielder could get to the ball, a pig ran out and swallowed it. Everyone stated arguing about the ruling on the play.

The umpire finally ruled that it was an inside-the-pork home run.

ROAR LINES, ROAR
★ Football ★

OFF DUTY

Marv Hubbard trotted back to the Oakland huddle after making a perfect block.

"How'd you like that block?" he asked quarterback Daryle Lamonica.

"Terrific," said Lamonica. "But you were supposed to carry the ball on that play."

Paul Brown began screaming when one of his tackles had two hunks of jersey torn off by the defensive end.

"That end was holding!" he yelled to the officials. "You gotta penalize him!"

The officials turned a deaf ear to his protests. The Bengals' coach glared at them.

"If that end didn't rip those holes out of his jersey," he grumbled, "it must have been moths."

PIKE'S PIQUE

Ohio State coach Woody Hayes is a hot tempered man. When things go wrong, he has to throw things. That usually means his watch. He'll rip it off his wrist, fling it to the ground, and stomp on it.

The players no longer worry about displays like this. They're used to it. When Woody did it again before the Michigan game one year, the players watched him silently for a moment. Then the high-pitched cackle of fullback Leon Lindsey cut through the air:

"Man, look at Woody! He's killin' time again!"

CATCHING DISEASE

Raider end Fred Biletnikoff has to have some of the best moves as well as best hands in pro football.

"That guy Biletnikoff catches passes the way the rest of

us catch colds," says his coach. "He knows where he gets some of them, and the others he just picks up in crowds."

GARRISON FINISH

Dallas fullback Walt Garrison doesn't go for fancy, frilly things. When the Cowboys voted to allow white shoes, he shrugged.

"Some guys think they're faster in white shoes. But tell me: if you put a white shoe on one foot and a black shoe on the other, would one leg be faster than the other?"

FRISKY COLT

Little, stumpy Don Nottingham is tough to bring down. When he lowers his head, you can hardly see him. After a Colt scrimmage, somebody asked linebacker Ray May how to tackle the fullback.

"You have to hit him low, very low," explained May, "somewhere around the neck."

TRUE LOVE

The TV football widow couldn't take it any more. Watching her husband hunched before his fourth televised game of the weekend, she sobbed, "You beast. You love football more than me!"

"Yes, dear," he replied, "but I love you more than basketball."

END OF THE LINE

On the first day of practice at Pearl River (New York) High School, Coach Pete Dyer asked one of his freshmen to go to the end of the blocking line. The boy came right back.

"I'm sorry, Coach," he said, "somebody is already there."

DEAD TO RIGHTS

George Allen sent a bouquet of roses to the telephone operators of the hotel he had stayed in for the Super Bowl game. The operators were thrilled.

"Thanks a million, Mr. Allen, we're so happy you appreciated our services."

"Appreciate?" snapped Allen, "I thought you were all dead."

TAKE A BRODIE

John Brodie had a terrible day against the Redskins. He couldn't hit a receiver. "After the game," he later admitted, "I tried to shoot myself . . . but the bullet was intercepted."

MAKE A WISHBONE

Indiana's coach Lee Corso knows that it is the players and not the formation that makes the offense.

At a press luncheon one day, a reporter raised his hand.

"Say, Coach," he asked, "are you going to use the Texas Wishbone T next season?"

"Absolutely," replied Corso. "Soon as Texas sends me all their players."

STATUE OF LIMITATIONS

Larry Csonka and Mercury Morris were arguing about an opposing linebacker.

"Well, he may not be the greatest," said Csonka, "but you have to admit that he's a steady player."

"Steady?" echoed Mercury. "If he were any steadier he'd have to be called a statue."

JIMMY CRACK CORN

Jim Garrett, assistant Giant coach, has a sharp, smart way of barking orders.

"Hey," a reporter observed one afternoon, "notice how much Garrett sounds like James Cagney?"

"Typical Giant luck," was the answer. "They need Jimmy Brown and they get Jimmy Cagney."

PAY-OLA

Jet center John Schmitt has a nightly radio show. His program always features this canned message:

"This is Joe Namath, folks, and I am not telling you to listen to the John Schmitt Show because he's such an outstanding player. And I am not telling you to listen because John is a friend of mine. I *am* telling you to listen because he is paying me to say so."

CARRYING CHARGE

Randy Vitaha went way up for a pass from Jim Plunkett, and was blasted by the corner back. He fell to the ground like a broken doll. Two trainers carried him off.

Up in the TV booth, Tom Brookshier turned to Tucker Frederickson.

"Say, Tuck, I bet you used to be involved in plays like that when you starred for the Giants."

"You're right, Tom."

"You used to hit like that, right, Tuck?"

"No, I used to be carried out like that."

UNITAS STATES

Johnny Unitas paused during a workout to stare at a large group of fans who were watching him.

"Look at those people," he said. "They're telling their kids, 'See that Unitas; you play football for 17 years and your body will look like that.'"

HAVING A BALL

A Nebraska back dove over the middle from the one-yard line. Just as he got to the goal line, he dropped the ball—which was recovered by Missouri.

Nebraska coach Ernie Bearg thought his man had scored before he fumbled. Referee Warren Giles ruled otherwise.

Bearg charged the referee. "How far over the goal does a man have to go to score a touchdown, *Mister* Giles?" he demanded.

"With or without the ball, *Mister* Bearg?" was the icy reply.

BELL RINGER

Referee Tommy Bell had been getting the business from Coach George Halas all afternoon. Finally he blew his whistle, and paced off ten yards against the Bears.

"What's that for?" roared Halas.

"For coaching from the sidelines."

"That proves you don't know what you're doing!" shouted the Bears' coach. "The penalty for illegal coaching is 15 yards."

"I know, *Mister* Halas," Bell replied. "But the kind of coaching you do is worth only ten yards."

COMIC TURN

The coach was annoyed at his fullback. All during the blackboard session, the player had sat in the corner reading a comic book.

The following Saturday found the fullback sitting on

the bench. He sat there for three full periods. In the middle of the fourth quarter, the coach finally called upon him.

"Warm up," he ordered. The fullback began doing knee bends and practice charges.

"Are you ready?" the coach asked tensely.

"Yes, sir!" panted the fullback.

"Good! Here's a comic book. Start reading!"

NAME GAME

"What's the new halfback's name?" asked the pro coach.

"Osscowinsinsiski," replied an assistant.

"Great! Put him in the lineup. I want to get even with that announcer in the TV booth."

LOSERS' HEAVEN

Johnny Majors worked hard to cure Pittsburgh of its losing complex. He drove the team from noon to twilight, then lectured them in the squad room.

During one of his lectures, he harped on the importance of tackle play. "Most games," he declared, "are lost just inside or just outside the tackles."

Looking up he saw one of his tackles snoozing in the back row. "Thomas!" he roared. "Where are most games lost?"

Quick as a flash, Thomas replied, "Right here at Pittsburgh, Coach!"

PICKUP

The most lopsided game in history was Georgia Tech's 220-0 clobbering of Cumberland. By the fourth quarter, Cumberland was praying for the clock to run out.

At one point, the Cumberland quarterback fumbled the ball, and it bounced toward the left halfback. Three Georgia Tech monsters bore down on the poor fellow, who shied away.

"Pick it up!" his quarterback yelled.

"Pick it up, my foot!" the halfback yelled right back. "*I* didn't drop it!"

SECOND THE MOTION

The first- and second-string Notre Dame teams were playing a practice game, and Coach Ara Parseghian was unhappy. His varsity just couldn't get moving. As Parseghian turned to speak to an aide, an official penalized the varsity five yards.

"What's that for?" Parseghian asked upon turning back to the game.

"For backfield in motion," answered the official.

"Great!" snapped Parseghian. "That's the first motion anyone's been able to detect in our backfield all day."

MIRACLE WORKER

While plugging up a hole, the linebacker smashed a finger. The team doctor rushed him into the dressing room, where he bandaged the injury.

"Doctor," moaned the player, "will I be able to play the guitar when my hand heals?"

"Absolutely," assured the doctor.

"You're wonderful, Doctor. I never could play the guitar before."

HUMPTY DUMPTY

The Giants once beat the Redskins, 14-7, without making a first down. In fact they chalked up only one yard rushing.

"One yard!" sobbed the Redskin coach. "I can make more yardage than that just by falling down."

BOTTOMS UP

Tennessee was about to face Alabama for the conference title. Coach Bob Neyland took aside his guard, Herman Hickman.

"Look, Herman," he said. "On defense I want you to get a yard and a half across the line and make piles."

Herman began making piles. But it didn't help. Alabama upset the favored Vols. Neyland, heartsick, went over to Hickman.

"What happened out there, Herman?"

"I did just what you told me, Coach. I got a yard and a half across the line and made piles."

"I told you to make piles," Neyland groaned, "but not to be at the bottom all the time."

HEAD-STARCH PROGRAM

At practice one day Larry Csonka messed up a couple of plays, and Coach Shula began giving him the works.

"Listen, Coach," the big Dolphin fullback said, "those linebackers think they're pretty smart, but after I hit 'em a couple of times they'll be just as dumb as I am."

SHARK TREATMENT

The Green Bay Packers were super in every way when they were coached by Vince Lombardi. They feasted on other teams' blunders.

As one Milwaukee sportswriter put it, "Making a mistake against the Packers is like bleeding near a shark."

BRAIN TRANSPLANT

The Chicago Bear tackle messed up his assignment on a punt. He backed up and the ball caught him squarely in the seat of his pants. The opposing end picked it up and ran it over for a touchdown.

Coach George Halas yanked the tackle. The player tried to hide at the end of the bench, but Halas sought him out.

"How are you, fella?" he asked.

"Why, fine, Coach," answered the tackle, surprised by his coach's kindly tone.

"Good," drawled Halas, "for a while I was afraid the kick might have damaged your brain."

George Allen is another coach who has strict rules. When he coached at Whittier College, he permitted no one to smoke.

As he walked into the locker room one day, one of his players froze against the wall, a lighted cigarette at his feet.

"What about that cigarette?" demanded the coach.

"You can have it," the player quickly said. "You saw it first."

DEE TRUTH

Dee Andros' eyes bulged when he saw Southern California rumble out to play Oregon State.

"Look at those guys!" he exclaimed. "They're so big that every time they run out on the field they make it tilt to one side!"

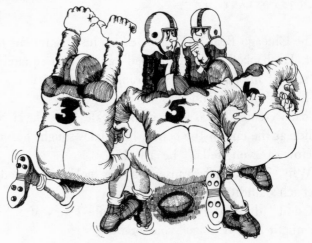

MENTAL PROBLEM

There's a quarterback in the NFL who can pass as well as Namath and Staubach, but just can't call a good game.

"He has an unusual brain," his coach explains. "It starts working the moment he gets up in the morning and doesn't stop until he gets into the huddle."

FORWARD THINKING

During a Wake Forest-Clemson game, the officials couldn't decide on a pass play. One ruled completion, the second ruled interception, and the third admitted he hadn't seen the play.

Referee Jack Lindsay wound up calling it incomplete.

"What else could I call it?" he explained. "A jump ball?"

ZERO HERO

The skinny young fellow had been on the squad for three years and had never gotten into a game. In the locker room after the last game, he was depressed. His girl friend had traveled 900 miles to see him play and he hadn't a bruise to show her.

Lost in thought he stumbled against the training table. A bottle of rubbing alcohol fell over and drenched the back of his pants. Unaware of this, he walked out to meet his girl friend. Suddenly he felt a trickle down his leg.

"Oh, Lord," he prayed, "I hope it's blood."

Boy Hayes, the great receiver, was needling Spider Lockhart, the Giants' safety man, at a banquet.

"I've always thought you were a nice guy," he told him.

"I don't get it," said Lockhart. "This is the first time we ever met."

"Sure, Spider, but I've passed you so many times going out for a pass that I feel like an old friend."

SHORT SNORTER

The ball was put down only six inches from the Oakland goal line. On the next play Cincinnati ran it over for a touchdown. The announcer informed the crowd that Doug Dressler had just scored on a six-inch run.

Up in the press box, a writer snorted, "How can you make a six-inch run?"

His neighbor grinned. "Well, after Dressler broke into the open, they couldn't catch him."

PIP TALK

The Yale coach knew he needed something extra against Harvard. He decided on a pep talk and gathered his squad around him.

"Men," he said, "I want you to remember what the letters of your school stand for. Y is for the Young men of Eli who will always rise to the occasion against Harvard. A is for Ambition, and that's what Yale men have always been noted for. L is for Loyalty, which all of us have for team and school. E is for the Effort all of us must exert today. Put 'em all together and they spell Yale! Now go out there and win! win! win!"

As the coach started for the door, confident that he had got his team sky-high, he overheard a lineman say to a back: "Gee, good thing we're not the Massachusetts Institute of Technology. We'd have been in there for another hour."

QUALITY OF MERCY

The student president at Indiana University demanded free football tickets for the returned prisoners of war. This made the local sports editor see red.

"I am against this," he wrote. "Those fellows have suffered enough already."

BLOODY MESS

Old Bob Zuppke was a great hand for pep talks. "Men," he bellowed one Saturday, "I want you to get in there and die for Illinois. Nobody will be taken out until he is dead. Get that—*dead*!"

Illinois played Ohio State to a standstill, until flesh gave out. Late in the final quarter, an Illini halfback keeled over from fatigue. Coach Zuppke grabbed a sub by the arm.

"Get in there for that man," he ordered.

The sub dashed out—then dashed right back.

"What's wrong?" shouted Zuppke. "Why didn't you take that man's place like I told you?"

"It wasn't necessary, Coach," gulped the sub. "He was still breathing a little."

BLOCK PARTY

Leaving the stadium after losing by a big score, the unhappy coach was grabbed by an old grad, who asked, "How many students are enrolled in our university?"

"About 21,000," replied the coach.

"Then why can't you get two of them in front of a ball carrier sometime?" snarled the old grad.

YOU GOTTA HAVE HART?

Watching Jim Hart throw eight straight passes without completing one, Coach Winner lost his cool.

"Jim," he snapped, "if it wasn't for the law of gravity, you couldn't even hit the ground."

CHOW HOUND

The big fullback had eaten his dinner and was now gazing with envy at a big steak that had just been placed before one of the defensive tackles.

"Hey, Marv," he said hopefully. "Don't tell me you're going to eat that big steak alone?"

"No," said the tackle, tucking his napkin under his chin, "with potatoes."

SPARTAN LIFE

Duffy Daugherty may be gone from Michigan State, but his jokes go marching on. After losing his fourth game in a row, he said, "There are a lot of teams in the country we can beat; unfortunately, we don't play them."

The Spartans faced Southern Cal, Notre Dame, and Michigan on successive weekends. Asked who had arranged the schedule, Duffy replied, "Not me. Our president has degrees from Johns Hopkins, Chicago, and Harvard, and I'm trying to get them on our schedule."

PEPPER STEAK

Pepper Rodgers was meeting his UCLA squad for the first time.

"Fellas," he said, "UCLA is a big place and I won't be able to check you closely. Be careful. Anyone so inclined can get into a lot of devilment right here on the campus."

A big tackle immediately raised his hand. "Where, Coach?"

PAUSE FOR REFRESHMENT

Sam Huff appeared on a TV show with O. J. Simpson. The great old linebacker began kidding the great young runner.

"I've seen you play a lot of times, O. J.," Huff said. "You're OK, but you're the razzle-dazzle type. In my day I'd have broken you in two."

"Buddy," O. J. drawled, "in your day you wouldn't have even broken my stride."

63

Minnesota had fumbled 19 times against Iowa and the coach was slowly going bananas. He ordered a backfield sub to warm up. The sub ran up and down the sideline and someone tossed him a ball. He dropped it.

A fan promptly yelled, "Send him in, Coach, he's ready."

LATE MOVIE

The coach of a major college team out west is still in shock. One evening his freshman star asked for $1,250 to go to a movie.

"Over a thousand bucks to see a movie?" gasped the coach. "Are you crazy?"

"No, Coach," explained the player, "it's a drive-in and I don't have a car."

NO-BUDDY AT HOME

Lance Alworth had had a tough game. He had dropped four passes and was booed off the field. After the game, he and a teammate walked out to the parking lot. Waiting there was Alworth's wife.

"Well, you still have one friend," said the teammate.

Alworth was touched. "Hello, dear," he said, holding out his arms—and accidentally dropping his car keys.

She went, "Boooooo!"

THAT'S THE TICKET

A weak team had held Northwestern to a tie. Coach Pont was fuming on the way to his car. A stranger tapped him on the shoulder.

"What's the matter with your team?" he snarled. "It stinks."

Coach Pont whirled on him. "Did you pay to get in?"

"Did I pay to get in?" The man held out a fistful of ticket stubs.

Pont nodded. "You're right, we stink."

JACK BE NIMBLE

Jack Kemp had a terrible year in his last season as Buffalo Bills' quarterback. Upon announcing his retirement, he said he was thinking of running for Congress.

"If Jackie throws his hat into the ring," a Buffalo columnist wrote, "you can bet that it will be intercepted."

BLOWIN' IN THE WIND

While training for the Super Bowl, Coach Vince Lombardi set an 11:30 P.M. curfew for his Packers. Several nights before the game, the coach went out for a late snack. He drove to a restaurant about four miles from the team's hotel. As he walked in, he ran smack into his star end, Max McGhee.

Lombardi glanced at his watch. It read 11:28.

"Max," he said coldly, "you know you're due back at the hotel."

"Not until 11:30, Coach."

"That gives you exactly two minutes. Do you think you can make it?"

McGhee mulled it over for a moment. "Not against this wind, Coach."

THE SOFT TOUCHE

As it turned out, Jack Kemp did throw his hat into the ring and he did get elected. Two years later he ran for re-election.

"Elect me," he warned the people in his district, "or I will come back as quarterback."

JOB INSECURITY

During their first six seasons, the Houston Oilers had five head coaches. It reached the point where the president of the club would leave the following instructions with his secretary:

"If the head coach calls while I am out, make sure to get his name."

BILL OF PARTICULARS

Coach Bill Peterson is a sort of Yogi Berra. Like Yogi,

he loses his grip on the language when he gets excited and says things like:

"We're all in this together, and don't you remember it."

"Men, I want you thinking of just one word all season. One word and only one word—Super Bowl."

"Don't you guys think for a minute that I'm going to take this loss standing down."

"Sometimes I feel like that psychiatrist, Frood."

PEAS AND KARRAS

Alex Karras wore thick glasses away from the football field. When he took them off to play, it left him almost blind. Yet he used to crush everyone he faced. One year he decided to try contact lenses.

His wife, Joan, described it this way: "Alex tried contact lenses for two games. They were sensational. Alex was so thrilled to see what was going on that he played the two worst games in his life."

GRIESE KID STUFF

Miami's great quarterback, Bob Griese, was leaving the stadium one Sunday when a stranger rushed up and grabbed him.

"Merlin Olsen!" the stranger cried. "Long time no see. My, how you've changed."

"I beg your pardon," Griese said.

"What's happened to you, Merl? You used to be six-five. Now you're only six feet."

"Look, buddy . . ." Griese started to protest.

"And you're so skinny! You used to weight 275. Now you can't weigh more than 200."

"Mister . . ." Griese protested.

"Look at your face, Merl. Where are those big apple cheeks you used to have? Now you look so drawn."

That did it. Griese grabbed the stranger's lapels and shouted, "Listen to me, bigmouth! I am not Merlin Olsen! I am Bob Griese!"

"What!" cried the stranger. "Changed your name, too!"

STRATEGY

The worried-looking stranger walked into the grocery store and ordered all the rotten eggs and overripe tomatoes in stock.

The clerk grinned. "I bet you're going to the football rally to hear Coach Brown."

"No," the customer sighed, "I am Coach Brown."

GOBBLE-DE-GOOK

The Oakland Raiders were astonished when a turkey showed up on the field and asked for a tryout. Coach Madden gaped as the turkey passed the ball 80 yards, kicked 55-yard field goals, and made three 65-yard dashes for touchdowns.

68

"You're sensational!" he told the turkey. "We'll give you a $50,000 bonus to sign with us for the season."

"Never mind the bonus," said the turkey. "Just promise to keep me after Thanksgiving Day."

SOCCER-TO-ME

Back in Knute Rockne's day, Notre Dame had the toughest football team in the land. One season Rockne decided to use soccer as a conditioner.

"The main idea of soccer," he explained to his squad, "is to kick the ball or kick the other fellow's shins."

The boys chose sides and lined up for the kickoff. That's when they discovered they had no ball. They thought it over for a moment, then a big lineman drawled:

"Heck with the ball, Coach. Let's start the game!"

CAR WASHOUT

The new pro coach had done a great job. He had lifted the team from a terrible 2-12 record to a championship 11-3. The club's owner decided to give him a surprise. He borrowed the coach's car and had it equipped with $1,500 worth of stereo equipment, a telephone, a hot plate, and a TV set.

He drove to the coach's house and tooted the horn. When the coach came out, the owner cried, "Look in your car, Chuck. All those extras are for you, for doing a great job! What do you think of it?"

"Gee, it's terrific," the coach sobbed. "But I forgot to tell you: It's a rented car."

LITTLE BY LITTLE

Fans who saw Floyd Little's snaky 85-yard punt return against the Lions swear that he must have covered at least 150 yards dodging in and out.

At one point, Little stopped short in front of the Lions' bench to let a would-be tackler fly past. The poor fellow landed at his coach's feet. Coach Schmidt looked down in disgust.

"Get up, sweetheart," he said, "that guy Little will be back in a minute."

ON THE FLY

It was the big game of the year. The Elephants were

leading the Fleas 17-14, when a Flea picked up a fumble and dashed 80 yards toward the goal. Just before he crossed the goal line, an Elephant came up and stepped on him.

As the stretcher bearers carried out the body, the Elephant's teammates scolded their clumsy teammate.

"Why weren't you more sporting? Why didn't you tackle the Flea instead of crushing him?"

"Honest, fellas," the Elephant sobbed. "I didn't mean to step on him. I only tried to trip him."

GREEN DREAM

The general manager of the Toronto Argonauts was trying to sign a young prospect from Grambling College. He began throwing around big numbers.

"What would you think, Willie, if you woke up tomorrow and found $100,000 in your pocket?"

"I'd think," replied Willie, "that I had put on Joe Namath's pants."

CHEERMEN OF THE BOARDS
★ Basketball ★

The high-school player was being interviewed for a scholarship by the coach of a state university.

"How's your outside shot?" asked the coach.

"Deadly."

"How are you on the inside?"

"My jumper is the greatest. I've got a great change of direction, and I can hook with either hand."

"What about your defense?"

"The best. Nobody has ever scored in double figures against me."

"Can you run?"

"I'm so fast I can grab the rebound, pitch out, then lead the fast break."

The coach shook his head. "Do you mean you haven't a single weakness?"

"Just a small one, Coach. I tell lies."

75

PLAYING IT COUSY

Bob Cousy put on a terrific show in a championship game—until, with two minutes to go, his wind gave out. Gasping for breath, he signaled for Coach Auerbach to take him out. The crowd gave him a standing ovation.

"Listen to that ovation!" said Auerbach.

"Ovation, my foot," groaned Cousy. "It's a eulogy. They think I'm going to die."

KAREEM OF THE CROP

Milwaukee's 7-foot-4 Kareem Abdul-Jabbar is so great that his coach, Larry Costello, claims, "You could cut him in two and he'd make a pair of All-American guards."

BLOCK PARTY

The Washington State scout was gushing over a high-school hotshot he had just seen.

"Is he quick?" asked head coach George Raveling.

"Quick?" echoed the scout. "He's so quick he can block his own shot!"

THE NUMBERS GAME

When the Atlanta Hawks signed Pete Maravich for close to $2 million, a reporter asked general manager Richie

Guerin what number was going to be assigned to the flashy superstar.

"With all the loot Maravich is getting, we'll probably give him an unlisted number," said Guerin.

PERSONAL STATIONARY

The star center had played a bad game. He had stuck to one spot on the floor and had wound up with only four points. As he left the court at the end of the game, a fan walked up to him and handed him a coin.

"What's this?" the player asked.

"It's the dime you played on all night, Stretch. You seemed so fond of it I didn't think you'd want to leave it on the court."

ALL OUR SUNS

In his first year as Phoenix Suns' coach, Johnny Kerr had a nightmare just before the opener against Seattle.

"I dreamed we'd go 0-82," he said.

The Suns won but it didn't help. "The next night I dreamed we'd go 1-81," moaned Kerr.

ONE ON ONE

The Villanova guard dribbled across the center line and was promptly belted by his man. Referee Steve Honzo quickly tooted his whistle for a foul.

The defensive man went into an act. "Who, me?" he squealed.

"Look around," said Honzo. "There's only you and me and it wasn't me."

FITCH TO BE TIED

George Mikan's son failed to make the Cleveland Cavaliers, and Coach Bill Fitch had to release him.

"Larry will be quite a player someday," Fitch told the press. "The trouble is he had terrible coaching in college."

"Who was his coach?" asked a writer.

"Me," replied Fitch.

HARDSHIP CASE

After the hopeless Cavaliers got bombed by the Lakers, Coach Fitch announced that high scorer John Johnson was coming out of the army as a hardship case.

"What kind of hardship?" Fitch was asked.

"Us."

HEIGHT OF MADNESS

Everyone got bug-eyed when Jacksonville took the floor at the NCAA championships several seasons ago. Imagine a starting lineup with a 7-foot-2 center, a 7-foot-0 and 6-foot-10 pair of forwards, and a 6-foot-5 guard! Only Evansville coach Arad McCutchan remained unimpressed.

"So what?" he said, "an 8-footer would murder them."

Big, skinny Johnny Ellis got involved in a pushing contest with Wilt Chamberlain. Johnny lost his head for a moment and made a threatening gesture at Wilt. The alert referee quickly threw his arms around Ellis.

"No! No!" screamed Ellis. "Don't hold me. Hold *him*!"

HE HITS THE SPOT

It was the first day of practice at Wingate High School in New York City. Coach Jack Kaminer handed a ball to each player.

"Fellas," he said, "I want you to practice shooting from the spots where you might expect to be in the game."

The number 12 sub immediately sat down on the bench and started arching the ball toward the basket.

SHAGGY PYGMY STORY

The goon center of the Pygmy Olympic Team was a shy guy who was sensitive about his height. Every morning he'd look into the mirror and sigh:

Mirror, mirror, on the wall
Who's the tallest man of all?
With everyone else just 2-foot-7,
Why must I be 3-foot-11?

CAUGHT ON THE REBOUND

Pete Newell's California teams were mighty proud of their defense—until the 1960 championship game against Ohio State. OSU hit 16 of its first 17 shots and missed only three during the entire half.

During the half-time break, Coach Newell told his team they would have to hit the boards harder.

"Darrel," he said to his All-American center, "you've got to get more rebounds off the defensive board."

"But, Coach," groaned the big fellow, "every ball I rebound has already gone through the hoop!"

AVERAGE SCHOLAR

One of those big-city high-school stars with a 65 percent shooting and a 45 percent grade average somehow managed to land a college scholarship. During his Christmas visit home, he went to see his old high-school coach.

"How are you doing?" his coach asked.

"Great! We have a terrific jayvee team and I'm averaging 19 points a game."

"How are you doing with the books?" the coach asked next.

"I'm doing great there, too, Coach. I've got a 1.2 average and all I need is a 2.4 to be eligible."

CRAZY, MAN

Driving to Atlanta for a game against the Hawks, Baltimore's coach, Gene Schue, stopped at a gas station. He noticed a figure shooting an imaginary basketball at an imaginary basket.

"What's that guy doing?" the Bullets' coach asked the attendant.

"Oh, don't pay any attention to him. He's slightly off his rocker. He used to be our high-school coach."

"Tell him to keep on shooting" replied Schue. "If we lose this game to the Hawks, I'll be back to guard him."

WHITE POWER

The coach's trademark was a white handkerchief. He waved it whenever he wanted his team to call a time-out.

One night his team was trailing by two points with time running out. The coach decided to stop the clock and plan a play. He waved his handkerchief.

Nobody noticed it. He waved it again. Nothing. He jumped to his feet and started waving it wildly.

A small boy behind the players' bench nudged his father. "Look, Dad," he said, "the coach is surrendering."

After Duke beat North Carolina in a weird slow-down game, an unhappy fan slumped into his living room.

"We lost 21-20," he told his wife.

"Too bad, dear," she murmured. "Who missed the extra point?"

MORTAL SILENCE

The coach had to leave the skull session to make a phone call. Upon returning he was astonished to find all his players sitting in complete silence.

"What a happy surprise!" he exclaimed. "Will someone give me an explanation for this?"

The team captain spoke up. "Sir, you once told us that if you ever left the room and came back to find everyone sitting perfectly still, you'd drop dead."

HAPPINESS IS . . .

The Detroit Pistons kicked off one season with a contest. The fans had to complete the following sentence in 25 words or less: "I like the Detroit Pistons because. . . ."

The winner turned out to be an 11-year-old boy. His entry read: "I like the Detroit Pistons because I do not live in Boston, New York, Milwaukee, Chicago, Philadelphia, or Baltimore."

Al McGuire blew up at practice one day.

"The boys shot so poorly today," he moaned to a reporter, "that when the janitor took the rim off the backboard to make some reapirs, the boys played 45 minutes before they missed it."

THE REAL DOPE

At a writers' luncheon, one of the reporters spotted a coach who hadn't had a winning season in five years.

"According to the preseason dope," the writer said, "your team ought to wind up in the NCAA tournament."

"Now, wait a minute," replied the shocked coach. "What is the name of the preseason dope who told you that?"

A GAME TRY

Long Island University was having an off-night against Seton Hall. During the half-time break, Coach Roy Rubin lashed into his players. He gave each one a going-over until he came to a sophomore named Sandy Rick.

"Sandy," he roared, "you look terrible tonight, too. What have you to say for yourself?"

"Only this, Coach: you haven't put me into the game yet."

GRAVE SITUATION

A player was trying to take the ball out along the crowded sideline, but his guard kept crowding him.

"Give him three feet," the referee shouted to the guard.

From the crowd came a voice. "Quiet, ref, or we'll give *you* six feet."

HAVING A BALL

Nate Archibald is a midget for a pro, standing just six feet tall. He spent his first two weeks as a rookie gaping at 6-foot-10 guys plucking rebounds off the roof.

"How do you like pro ball?" Coach Bob Cousy asked one night.

"I don't know, Coach," Archibald replied. "The ball hasn't come down to me yet."

SHOE-PRIZE PACKAGE

The St. Bonaventure equipment manager gulped when the great Bob Lanier reported.

"Do you have a uniform?" he asked, looking in awe at Lanier's 6-foot-11 frame and 250-pound body.

"Everything but the shoes," answered Bob.

"I'll dig up a pair. What size do you wear?"

"Fifteen or sixteen," Lanier blushed. "But make it 15s, huh. I don't want to look conspicuous."

Only one second remained in the third quarter when Fred Carter grabbed the ball off the defensive board. All the 76er guard could do was whirl and heave the ball 94 feet toward the other basket. He almost brained a photographer squatting along the end line.

Knick scout Dick McGuire, sitting in the press section, threw up his hands.

"How can a guy miss a shot like that?" he deadpanned.

GARBAGE DISPOSAL

It was Bill Bridges Night in Atlanta. Since the mayor couldn't make it, he had his vice-mayor, Maynard Jackson, sub for him. The vice-mayor explained that the mayor was tied up in the municipal workers strike.

"Mayor Massell is out trying to get the garbage collected," Jackson told the crowd. "He suggests that when you are finished with your paper cups and cardboard boxes, please eat them."

BIG DEAL

Looking for a little publicity one day, the owner of the Hawks offered the Lakers $2 million for Elgin Baylor.

This made the Hawks' coach gasp.

"When I heard my owner was offering $2 million for Baylor," he said, "I thought he meant Baylor University."

Mendy Rudolph, the crack pro official, was supposed to take a train from Atlanta to Boston.

"Too rough," he grumbled. "I think I'll fly in tomorrow. I'm not going to ride a coach all night."

"Why not?" snapped his wife. "Don't the coaches ride you all night?"

ANXIOUS MOMENT

The coach put the eager young sub into the game early in the fourth quarter, and the kid went wild. He sank eight long shots in a row, pulling his team ahead. He then called time and ran over to the bench.

"Coach," he asked, "do you think I'm shooting too much?"

RIGHT GUARD

About the only player who could do a decent job of guarding Wilt Chamberlain was Bill Russell. He explained it this way:

"Wilt could do just about everything. So I used a three-part defense against him. One, I tried to keep him away from the ball. Two, if that failed, I tried to stay between him and the basket."

Russell would pause at this moment, and the listener would naturally ask, "And what was three?"

"Three," Russell would grin, "was when everything else failed—I'd panic."

GOT HIS NUMBER

The Celtics program used to carry lucky numbers for which prizes were awarded. One night the Celtics were being drubbed by the Lakers, and Coach Auerbach saw red. He flung his rolled-up program away.

A fan promptly yelled, "Better keep it, Red. You might win the radio."

SHOOTING FOR THE STARS

Seven-year-old Jimmy had been taught that Sunday was a day for prayer, not play. So his mother was surprised to find him practicing pivot shots in the backyard.

"Jimmy," she scolded, "don't you know it's wicked to play ball on Sundays?"

"Oh, that's all right, Mother," he explained. "This isn't pleasure. I'm practicing shooting against Abdul-Jabbar."

SAY IT WITHOUT MUSIC

Adolph Rupp used to tell people that the Coliseum in Lexington, Kentucky, was a war memorial, not a basketball arena. But one afternoon his varsity took the floor—only to have an official run up to them.

"You can't practice here," he said. "Artur Rubinstein is rehearsing for a piano concert and he must have silence."

"Nonsense!" bellowed the Kentucky coach. "Rubinstein can play tonight and miss a hundred notes and nobody will know the difference. But let one of my players miss a shot and the whole world will know about it. We're gonna practice."

WHERE THERE'S A WILT

When Wilt Chamberlain played for Kansas, his coach would often bench him in order to keep the score down. Against Missouri one evening, the coach benched him with the score 61-43. Missouri closed the gap to 65-57 in the closing moments. A young Missouri fan turned to her boyfriend.

"We're doing all right, huh?" she beamed.

"Yeah, but I hope we don't do any better," sighed the boyfriend. "Or they'll put Chamberlain in again."

WELL-DONE TREAT

"I'm fed up with rookies and green kids," an NBA coach complained to Red Holzman, the Knicks' coach. "Can you trade me a finished ball player?"

"I've got two who are all finished," replied Red. "Which do you want?"

Back in the old days, Oklahoma State played a very slow kind of offense. The Aggies mothered the ball and refused to shoot until they were wide open. Against Kansas one night, the Aggies could do nothing right. They fell 20 points behind—but still kept "sitting" on the ball.

Toward the end of the game an Aggie took a pass around the foul line. He looked at the basket, brought the ball up for a shot. Then he lowered the ball, looked around uncertainly, and brought the ball up again.

A fan finally lost patience.

"Shoot, darn it!" he screamed. "You got the wind with you!"

SMOKE SCREEN

The teams that play in the National Invitational Tournament in Madison Square Garden love to rib one another. When St. Joseph's of Philadelphia visited town, the St. John's boosters held up a poster that read:

"Philly isn't a city; it's a cigar."

When Holy Cross came to the Garden, its pep squad walked around the court carrying two huge, colorful signs.

One sign read: "Foley-O'Connor-Kelley-McClory-Slattery."

The other read: "Palace-Canavan-Gallagher-Jordan-Foley."

Following them closely was a group carrying a third sign: "Wall-to-Wall Irishmen."

The Philadelphia 76ers of 1972-73 could have been the worst team in pro basketball history. At one stage of the season they were something like 4-51.

One night everything suddenly fell into place. They ran up a 15-point lead. One of the fans went out of his mind. And when Tom Van Arsdale sank a jumper to put the 76ers 17 points up, the fan found it too much.

"Take a time out, Philadelphia," he roared. "I gotta go out for a shock treatment!"

TWO-BIT TOWN

The veteran pro referee, Joe Gushue, took his son, Michael, to a game in Detroit. Late in the game one of Gushue's calls angered the fans. Some of them threw pennies onto the court. Gushue scooped them up, walked over to the sideline, and gave them to his son.

"This town is bush," his son said scornfully. "In Baltimore they throw quarters."

RUPP AND READY

There never was a greater coach than Adolph Rupp. Nor a tougher one. The Kentucky coach played the game to the hilt.

In one game he kept yelling instructions to his boys. Finally the ref called a technical foul on him for coaching from the bench. After the game Rupp was asked for his opinion of the ref's action.

"It didn't bother me," was the surprising answer. "My coaching is worth a technical foul anytime."

THE SPANISH MAIM

For excitement and noise, it's tough to beat basketball in Spain. The fans get so excited they drown out the ref's whistle. The whistle toots. But the teams go right on playing, until there's a slight lull. Then the ref goes over to the scorers' table and says:

"The last six baskets didn't count."

CHEERFUL EARFUL

The principal of the school was giving the young coach some advice on the first day of practice.

"You'll discover that at nearly every skull session some player will be eager to argue. Your first thought will be to silence him. Think carefully before you do. He'll probably be the only one listening."

TOKENS OF ESTEEM

The team had gone undefeated and won the state championship. At the victory banquet the following week, the school superintendent turned to the coach and said,

"Coach Weber, how can we ever show our appreciation?"

"Sir," replied the coach, "ever since the ancient Phoenicians invented money, there has been only one answer to that question."

WHAT'S NUDE?

The little play-maker drove down the middle—and felt something snap. Before he could reach down, his pants dropped to his ankles.

"Poor guy," remarked the scorer, "he reminds me of a newborn baby."

"How come?" asked the timer.

"He's small, he's red, and he needs help."

FLASH IN THE PAN

The unhappy college player was describing his coach to his roommate.

"He's a great planner," the player explained. "He takes great pains with everything . . . and then gives them to the rest of us."

BOOS-HOO

He was the worst player on the team. For close to four years he sat on the bench without getting to play. One night late in his senior year, it happened. Three players had fouled out and the game was hopelessly lost. The coach looked down the bench.

"Billy, go in for Jack," he called.

The fans started booing as the player checked in. The coach felt terrible. He walked over and put his arm around the sub.

"Don't pay any attention to those people, Billy," he told him.

The boy looked at him in surprise.

"Now wait a minute, Coach," he said. "They're not booing me—they're booing *you* for putting me in."

AH, SWEET MISTER I. OF LIFE

Hank Iba coached for 40 years at Oklahoma State, and he also coached three U.S. Olympic teams. In that time, no player ever dared call him anything but Mr. Iba. He was very fair and honest—and strict.

At a class reunion one spring, two of his old players met for the first time in years. They began telling stories about their old coach.

"I just had a son and I named him after Mr. Iba," said one.

"Named him Henry, eh?" said the other.

"Nope, named him Mister."

COUNT-DOWN

Mel Counts kept missing shot after shot in practice. His coach finally blew his top. He grabbed the big fellow by the shirt, shoved his face up into his chin, and growled, "Mel, I'm going to get you so mad you're going to take a punch at me." He then let Mel go. "It's no use," he said sadly. "With your eye you'd probably wind up hitting the bleachers."

HORSE LAUGH

When 6-foot-9 Johnny Kerr arrived in Phoenix to coach the Suns, he ran into a little old lady in the street. She looked the huge red-headed fellow up and down and shook her head.

"Did you ever play basketball?" she asked.

"No, ma'am," drawled Kerr. "I was a jockey for a dinosaur."

BIG-TIME SPENDER

It was a rough game for the 76ers. One player picked up

94

a $25 fine for fighting. Another was fined $25 for swearing at a fan. And the coach, Dolph Schayes, picked up another $25 fine for making an unfriendly remark to the referee.

In the locker room after the game, Schayes looked happy. "It was a $500 night for us," he laughed.

One of the players quickly figured that the three $25 fines came to only $75. "How do you figure $500?" he asked.

"I'm a big tipper," explained Schayes.

BAR ASSOCIATION

The sophomore star complained to his coach during a time-out, "The ref is giving us the business. He's a crook!"

"Come, come, Joey," chided the coach. "The ref is completely honest. He happens to be a member of the bar."

"I knew it!" said the player. "I could smell it on his breath!"

MULTIPLE CHOICE

Jack Donahue coached Lew Alcindor at Power Memorial Academy. After Alcindor graduated and went to UCLA, Donahue became coach at Holy Cross College.

In one of his first games at Holy Cross, his team fell behind by 30 points. A voice came floating from the gallery.

"Hey, Donahue, why don't you go back to high school?" Then, "Hey, Donahue, why don't you get Alcindor?"

"My athletic director is a wonderful man," Donahue told the reporters after the game. "He told me that either one was OK with him."

TEAMWORK

The team had just lost a game by 65 points, and the coach was asked for a comment.

"It was just a team effort," he said.

PRACTICE MAKES IMPERFECT

The bench warmer hadn't scored a point all season. With seconds to go in the last game, the coach put him in.

As luck would have it, he was immediately fouled. He went to the free-throw line for two shots. He shot the first—and it didn't even reach the basket. The captain walked over to steady him.

"Relax, Mike," he whispered. "Shoot just like you do in practice."

"But, Bob," the sub whispered back. "I always miss in practice."

SLAVE DRIVER

The high-school team had done the impossible. They had upset three big teams and were now going to play for the state title. The excited coach and his assistant were driving to the state university for the championship game.

As their car entered the big city, the coach started to pour out directions. "Go two blocks, then turn to the right; go four more blocks and turn to the left; then make a slight turn on the next corner and make a right; drive four more blocks and. . . ."

"But, Coach," groaned his assistant, "you're driving!"

YOUNG AND OLD

During the 1970 NBA playoffs, Dick Young took one look at the Lakers' starting lineup and wrote:

"Wilt Chamberlain is 33, Jerry West is 32, Elgin Baylor is 35, and right about now, in this 108th game [of the season] their coach sits just outside Shangri-la, watching them turn to wrinkles in his arms."

WAY OVERTIME

Back in 1949 the Nats and Packers played five overtime periods. The game ran well past midnight. During the fifth overtime, Nat forward George Ratkovicz came over to the scorers' table.

"How many personals do I have?" he asked.

"Four."

"Four?" yelled George. "A few minutes ago you told me three."

"That," said the scorer, "was *yesterday*."

John Erickson, formed Wisconsin coach, once told a group of writers that he had turned down Lew Alcindor (now Abdul-Jabbar).

"I told Lew that I wouldn't take him until he took back what he had said about Wisconsin."

"What did he say?" asked an unbelieving reporter.

"Lew said, 'I won't come.' " grinned Erickson.

TIME KILLER

Few of the reporters at the NBA All-Star Game could understand the big, crowded scoreboard clock. One of them finally yelled, "I can't tell the darned time."

A fan in the front row promptly yelled back, "It's easy, dummy. The little hand is for minutes and the big hand is for hours."

TO BE FRANK

South Carolina's coach, Frank McGuire, is now one of the aristocrats of the business. But he never has forgotten his humble beginnings.

"I came from such a poor neighborhood," he says, "that when my mother tossed the dog a bone he always had to signal for a fair catch."

A LITTLE TWIT

OF EVERYTHING
★ Other Sports ★

SILENCE IS GOL-DARN

The two golf rivals, Doc and Jack, argued so much they finally agreed not to talk at all during a match.

All went smoothly and silently until the sixteenth hole. There Doc walked up to a ball on the edge of the green, while Jack climbed into a sand trap.

Jack took one swing, then another, and another, and still another. Finally he hit the ball clear across the green and into a trap on the other side. From there he whanged the ball back into the first trap.

As he wearily recrossed the green, Doc broke the long silence.

"May I say a word?" he asked.

"Well," snarled Jack, "what is it?"

"You're playing my ball."

FOUL PLAY

After lofting a tee shot which fell about 20 feet in front of the tee, the beginning golfer shook his head.

"Gentlemen," he said, turning to his partners, "I have a hen who can lay an egg farther than that."

COLD CUT

When Madison Square Garden put in its cooling system, the public-address announcer made a big fuss about it. At a fight one hot July night, he proudly announced:

"Ladies and gentlemen, I'd like to inform you that the temperature outside is 95. In here it is 65."

While he paused to let this thought sink in, a loud voice came out of the dark:

"Yeah, and don't forget it's nothing outside and 25 bucks in here."

NO DRIVE

A woman golfer was having a bad time. After flubbing an easy shot, she turned on her grinning caddy.

"If you don't stop grinning," she screeched, "you'll drive me out of my mind."

"That wouldn't be a drive, ma'am," he said, "only a putt."

FOR WHOM THE BELL TOLLS

The ham-and-egg fighter took a sock on the jaw and crumbled to the canvas. The referee bent over him and started to count. At six he noticed that the boxer's eyes were open.

"Do you intend to fight any more?" he asked.

"You bet, Mister Referee," was the reply, "but not tonight."

CUP CAKE

The golf pro took the woman up to the tee. He pointed to the distant green and said, "Drive the ball as near to the flag as you can."

The woman took a crazy swing, but, as luck would have it, sent the ball just two feet from the cup!

"What do I do next?" she asked the pro.

"You knock it into the hole," the pro explained.

"Into the hole?" she shouted. "Why didn't you tell me that in the first place!"

NICE BERG

The old British lightweight, Jackie (Kid) Berg, was an ultrapolite gentleman. One day he was taking a beating, and his trainer, Ray Arcel, kept wondering what was holding him up. As Jackie staggered to his corner after the round, Arcel grabbed him and said, "Jackie, Jackie, how do you feel?"

"Fine," politely murmured Berg, "and you?"

EGG BEATER

Jim Ryun's wife had broken her kitchen timer. "Jim," she called to the famous distance-runner, "there's only one way I can time your egg—run out and do the mile."

SLOW MOTION

Ken Gibson, the Kentucky State College track coach, watched one of his hopeless athletes running the mile.

"That boy is so slow," he remarked, "that if he ever got caught in the rain, he'd rust to death."

ARTIST AT WORK

The boxing manager got a call from a small-time promoter. The latter needed a heavyweight fighter for a match in Worcester.

"I've got just the fellow for you," said the manager, "18 fights, 18 knockouts."

"Great!" cried the promoter. "But, gee, I don't want him beating up our local hero."

"Don't worry," the manager assured him.

After the fight, the promoter phoned the manager: "A terrible thing happened. Your fighter was knocked out."

"Don't worry," said the manager, "19 fights, 19 knockouts."

MAD-CAP

The coach lost a big game by his own dumb mistakes. Next day his wife was doing a little shopping when she was approached by an angry fan.

"Does your husband suffer from insanity?" inquired the fan.

"Of course not," replied the wife. "He enjoys every minute of it."

TAIL GUNNER

The athletic director of Clemson University was asked to start a rowing team. A football man from way back, the A. D. roared:

"Clemson will never offer a sport where a man sits on his tail and goes backward!"

AYES OF TEXAS

"The only thing bigger than the Houston Astrodome," boasted a happy Texan, "is outside."

OPEN SEASON

An old lady was watching Lee Trevino loft one high-arching golf shot after another in practice.

"Beautiful!" she yelled. "Beautiful!"

The Texan gave her a pained look.

"Lady," he said, "so what did you expect from the National Open champion—ground balls?"

MOUTH TRAP

The Sunday golfer was trying to blast his way out of a trap. He moaned, whined, then cried to his partner, "These traps are darned annoying!"

"You're right," was the reply. "So why don't you close yours?"

ICE CREAMED

Detroit hockey fans went into shock when the Maple Leafs whitewashed the Red Wings 13-0—the worst defeat in Detroit's history. Only star player Alex Delvecchio kept his cool.

"It could have been worse," he figured. "Suppose we hadn't blocked the kick after Toronto's second touchdown?"

RACE PREJUDICE

The average sports fan never gets excited about the America's Cup (yachting) race. After all it is not a widely popular sport. Yet the TV and newspaper coverage rivals the World Series.

It was John Lardner who put the event in its proper place: "All America's Cup races should be held on the Niagara River, with the start just above the falls."

Baseball great Hank Aaron was introduced to golf great Jack Nicklaus.

"What kind of golfer are you?" Nicklaus asked.

"Terrible," replied Aaron. "It took me 17 years to get 3000 hits in baseball, and only one afternoon to do it in golf."

MONEY SAVER

The pretty young girl informed her golf instructor she was switching sports.

"What are you switching to?" asked the pro.

"Bowling," was the answer.

"Bowling!" howled the pro. "How can you like it better than golf?"

"It's cheaper," replied the girl. "Last night I bowled three hours and didn't lose a ball."

LIKE A ROCKET

Montreal's all-time hockey hero had to be Maurice (Rocket) Richard. Toward the end of his career, he used to help with the broadcasts. He would pick the three stars of the game, which is the custom in Canada. Poor Rocket had a hard time forgetting his loyalty to his beloved Canadiens.

One night, after a Canadien-Red Wing game, Richard

picked his three stars and brought them over to the microphone.

"For ze first star, I pick Jean Beliveau of Canadiens. He scored a goal, set up another, and played a strong game.

"For ze second star, I pick Dickie Moore, also of Canadiens. He also scored a goal and assisted on Beliveau's goal."

"And the third star?" the announcer asked, looking for Richard to pick one of the visitors.

"Ze third star is my brother Henri," said Richard. "He didn't score, but he was all over ze ice."

The announcer, all shook up, tried to save the day. "If you had to name one Red Wing as a star, who would it be?"

"Well," Richard replied, "if there was one Red Wing who stood out, it would be Gordie Howe. If he hadn't scored those four goals, ze Canadiens would have won."

WHAT'S IN A NAME?

What happens when parents name a boy Lancelot Galahad? You're right. The poor boy has to fight for his life every day. And that's exactly what happened to Lancelot Galahad Nuzzpickel.

One afternoon his teacher brought him home with a bloody nose and a black eye. The teacher knocked on the door and Mr. Nuzzpickel opened it.

"Mr. Nuzzpickel," the teacher said wearily, "why don't you change Lancelot Galahad's name? Otherwise he's going to have to fight somebody every day."

"Great!" beamed Mr. Nuzzpickel. "I want him to be a boxer, and that name gets him a lot of free practice."

GAME TO THE CORE

Billy Cunningham, the great basketball player, talked Arnie Palmer into playing a round of golf with him. Eighteen holes later, Cunningham asked the obvious question, "What do you think of my game, Arnie?"

"Not bad," nodded Palmer, "but I still prefer golf."

SICK TO THE STOMACH

The fighter was so beat up there didn't seem any way he could come out for the next round. His manager worked over him feverishly in the corner.

"Butch, Butch, just hang in there for one more round," he begged. "I can see what that guy is doing to you is beginning to sicken him."

THE GOOD LORD

Lord Killanin, the president of the International Olympic Committee, is something of a wit. He was holding a meeting one day when a committee member came rushing in, full of apologies for being late.

"Blame it on Pan Am," he puffed.

"Please," said Lord Killanin, "no advertising."

LORD'S PRAYER

A reporter asked a priest, "What would the Lord do if two teams prayed for victory with exactly the same fervor?"

The priest's eyes twinkled. "I imagine," he said, "that He would just sit back and enjoy a whale of a game."

THE LETTER-BUG

The proud father was bragging about his son, a great all-round athlete but a dunce in the classroom.

"My boy won his fourth letter this winter," he boasted to his business partner.

"Very true," replied the other quietly, "but I bet you had to read it to him."

GUM(P) DROP

When Gump Worsley was tending net for the then pathetic Rangers, he was asked to name the team that gave him the most trouble.

"That's easy," he immediately replied, "the Rangers."

ONE THAT GOT AWAY

After owning a horse for eight years, a sportsman decided to enter him in a race. Having no record, the nag went off at 90 to 1. He zoomed around the track and won by 12 lengths. The officials called in the owner.

"How come you never raced this horse before?" they demanded. "After all, you've had him for eight years."

"To tell the truth," the owner replied, "we couldn't catch him until he was seven."

RABID DELIVERY

After being bitten by a stray dog, the coach learned that it was rabid. He promptly whipped out a pad and began writing.

"What are you doing?" asked his startled doctor.

"Just making a list of the alumni I'm going to bite," replied the coach.

STRING FEVER

The sportswriter, covering his first tennis tournament was astounded to see a player swinging at the ball with a banjo.

"Good lord!" he yelled to the umpire. "Why don't you tell him he's supposed to use a racket!"

"We can't now," the umpire replied. "He's just reached the semifinals."

PIECE WORK

The athletic director was checking on the references of a new coach.

"How long did Tony work for you?" he asked the coach's old boss.

"Oh, about eight hours," was the answer.

"Eight hours!" exclaimed the A. D. "He told me he was with you for four years."

"He was, he was," answered the old boss.

DOUBTING THOMAS

John Thomas was rated the world's number 1 high jumper until he came up against Valeri Brumel. The Russian beat him in the 1960 Olympics and then outjumped him every time they met in later meets.

Preparing for the 1964 season, Thomas was asked how he felt about all those beatings.

"If I hadn't lost to Brumel so often," he said, "I wouldn't know what I know now."

"And what do you know now?" he was asked.

"How to be a good loser," grinned Thomas.

Bruce Weber is one of America's greatest sports fans. He explained this carefully to the girl he was about to marry.

"I love sports and I'll watch anything, even water polo."

"*Water* polo?" she wondered. "How in the world do they ever get the horses into the pool?"

ALL WET

After becoming a star in the movies, swimming champ Esther Williams admitted that it wasn't her acting but her swimming ability that put her on top.

A critic put it this way: "Wet, she's a star. Dry, she isn't."

HIT PARADE

The duffer finally hit a drive within distance of the green and eagerly turned to his caddy. "Do you think I can reach it with a six?"

The bag-toter nodded his head gravely. "If you hit it often enough, sir."

WHEN FORE IS A CROWD

Hubby was a golf nut. His wife was bugged on auction sales. Both talked in their sleep. In the middle of the night, he would yell "Fore!" and she would answer "Four-and-a-quarter!"

CLOCK-WATCHER

After his ninth knockdown, the boxer looked all out. From the corner his manager yelled, "Stay down! Stay down until eight!"

Lifting his head from the canvas, the fighter wearily asked, "What time is it now?"

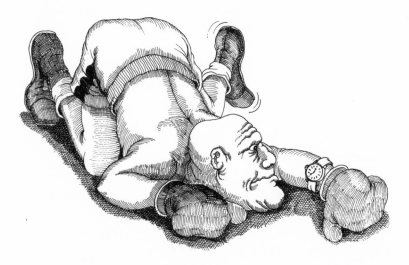

COURSE FELLOW

The duffer was brought into the hospital suffering from sunstroke. As the nurse began reading his temperature, "102-103-104," the suffering sportsman raised his head. "Sweetie," he whispered, "what's par for this hospital?"

The stuck-up society woman walked away from the eighteenth hole, her nose high in the air.

"I went around in 76," she announced.

To which a rival coldly answered, "With Paul Revere, no doubt."

TEE FOR THREE

John McKay, the USC football coach, was playing golf with his assistant coach. He was about to hit a wood shot, when his assistant stopped him.

"Don't hit from there, Coach," he said. "That's the ladies' tee. The men's tee is about 50 yards behind you."

"Look, my friend," said McKay, "I'd like you to know that it took me *three strokes* to get here."

LIKE IKE

Former President Eisenhower was putting on his spikes for a game of golf.

"Dad," asked his son John, "have you noticed anything different since you left the White House?"

"Yes," smiled Ike, "a lot more golfers are beating me."

HAVE HOPE

Bob Hope is one of the world's best-known golfers. After

playing a round with Spiro T. Agnew, he reported, "The Vice-President plays very well. As a matter of fact, he beat me. Of course I had to shoot 136 to do it."

A LOT OF BULL

Joe Garagiola was showing his friend Harry Caray around his recreation room. Noticing a deer's head above the fireplace, Caray remarked, "I didn't know you were a big-game hunter, Joe."

"I'm not," explained Garagiola. "The deer was given to me for making an after-dinner speech."

"You know," said Caray, "you're probably the first guy who ever shot the bull and got a deer."

WATCH ON THE RYUN

Jim Ryun, the great miler, was being kidded by a reporter.

"You like to do a lot of different things in your training, so why don't you go out for football?"

"That may be a good idea," grinned Ryun. "But I think I'll stick to track. I'll probably be better off in the long run."

ANCHORS AWAY

Back in his teen-age days, Olympic swimming coach George Haines was a struggling swimmer. The best you could say of him was that he managed to forge steadily ahead.

His first 1500-meter race was a disaster. The coach took him aside.

"George," he said, "your stroke is beautiful, but you have a slight fault: You stay in one place too long."

BAR AND GRILL

Before coming to the United States for a series of meets, Valeri Brumel cleared 7-feet-4½ inches from a dirt takeoff in Leningrad.

"Were you surprised to clear that height?" he was asked by an American writer.

"Not at all," Brumel replied.

"How much over the bar were you when you cleared it?"

Brumel smiled. "I had no time to look."

SWEET SUE

The seven-year-old girl was in a gym for the first time in her life. She immediately began trying out all the apparatus. When she came to the horizontal bar, she decided to make like Olga Korbut. Sure enough she fell off and landed on her back. A pained expression crossed her face.

The teacher picked her up, cradled her in her arms, and said soothingly, "Go ahead and cry, child, cry all you want."

"Cry?" the little girl said. "Heck! I'm going to sue somebody."

As astronaut Walter Schirra was reentering earth some years ago, the Dodgers were kicking and fumbling the ball around in a playoff game against the Giants.

"It's a good thing that Schirra wasn't dropped at Chavez Ravine," wrote one reporter. "Nobody would have picked him up."

TEST CASE

The editors of the *City College Alumnus* invited John Kieran to write an article about his sports activities as a student many years before.

"I became a varsity fancy diver," he told them, "as a result of a chemistry exam."

"How could a chemistry exam make you a varsity diver?" he was asked.

"Because," Kieran explained, "the two regular divers flunked and had to be dropped from the team."

OH, SAY, CAN YOU SEA?

In the Sahara Desert, two travelers stopped their jeep beside a man who was trotting along in bathing trunks.

"I'm on my way to have a swim," he explained.

"But the sea is more than 500 miles away!" the driver exclaimed.

"500 miles away?" said the bather. "I say isn't this a splendid beach!"

CHESS IN CASE

A man and a dog were sitting around a table playing chess. The woman of the house came in and almost fainted at the sight.

"Why, that's the most amazing thing I have ever seen —a dog playing chess!"

"What's so wonderful?" barked the dog. "I haven't won a game yet."

KILLER-DILLER

Joe Louis gave Max Baer a terrible licking before knocking him out. Baer took a lot of ribbing about that kayo.

"Kid me all you like," Baer said to his friend, Jack Dempsey, "but just the same I gave Louis a terrific scare."

"You sure did," agreed Dempsey. "For a while he must have thought he killed you."

120

St. Peter and St. Thomas Aquinas were playing golf. St. Peter stepped up on the first tee and banged one 525 yards for a hole-in-one. St. Thomas then took his turn—and did the same thing.

They moved to the second tee, where St. Peter hit a 635-yard drive straight into the hole. St. Thomas stepped up and *bang*—also a hole in one. They covered the first nine holes in this fashion, matching ace for ace.

On the tenth hole, St. Peter turned to St. Thomas.

"What do you say, Tom, shall we cut out the miracles and play golf?"

COME-BACKER

A boy talked his father into buying him a boomerang. He practiced until he became an expert with it. When his birthday came around, all he wanted was a new boomerang.

Several weeks later a family friend heard that the boy had been placed in a mental institution. He called up the father.

"What happened?" he asked.

The father groaned. "You remember I got him a new boomerang for his birthday? Well, he went out of his mind trying to throw the old one away."

GOING DOWN

Luis Pires fought George Foreman some years ago. "Did you go down when he hit you?" he was asked.

"With Foreman in front of me, the ropes behind me, and the law of gravity keeping me from going up," was the answer, "where else could I go?"

ALI BABBLE

The fighter looked just like Muhammad Ali. The same face. The same body. The same fancy footwork.

"If I ever get Ali into the ring, nobody will be able to tell us apart," he boasted to a sportswriter.

"Everyone will be able to tell in a minute," replied the writer.

"How?" asked the unbelieving fighter.

"The one standing up will be Ali."

KNOCK ON WOOD

Tim Wood, a senior-high-school student from Indianapolis, broke the world record for sit-ups. He did 15,525 in a row in ten hours.

"What are you going to do now?" he was asked afterward.

"Go to the bathroom," he snapped.

STICKY WICKET

Annette Weber dreams up wild interviews. Her favorite is about a college polo coach. A reporter asks, "How are your prospects for next season, Coach?"

And the coach replies, "Terrible. All the players will be back, but the horses are graduating."

Randy Neumann is the new breed of prizefighter. He is handsome, clean-cut—and a straight A student at Fairleigh Dickinson University. His ambition is modest.

"I don't expect to be champ. I don't want to be a millionaire. I just want to be like Jerry Quarry—make $200,000 a fight."

TAYLOR-MADE

Chris Taylor, the 350-pound wrestling champ, is a wit. He has a crack for every occasion. He saves his big one for people who ask if he ever served in the army.

"No," he says, "when I went for my physical they rejected me."

"Too heavy?"

"No, too good-looking."

STROKE OF MIDNIGHT

Buck Dawson directs the Swimming Hall of Fame. He is also married to the daughter of Matt Mann, who may have been the greatest swimming coach of all time. The Manns are considered the royal family of swimming.

Son-in-law Buck is the black sheep of the clan.

"They are not sure whether I'm an in-law or an outlaw," he tells everyone. "And they have laid down a rule: I must do my swimming after dark so that nobody can see my stroke."

FLAW POLISH

Golfer Jimmy Demaret was playing with Spiro Agnew. After watching the Vice-President tee off, Demaret remarked, "Mr. Agnew, I believe you have a slight swing in your flaw."

JAY WALKER

Jay Crampton is the five-year-old son of Australian golf champ Bruce Crampton. He is very blond, very cute, very busy, and everyone is always making a fuss over him.

He was standing by the scoreboard one day when one of the woman scorers began *oohi*ng and *ahhi*ng over him.

"And whose little boy are you?" she asked.

Jay thought for a moment. "Arnold Palmer's," he said.

"And who is your favorite golfer?"

"Jack Nicklaus," was the reply.

LOST IN THE ROUGH

The two golfers went crazy playing behind a pair of female slowpokes. The women stopped to chat, pick flowers, and admire the scenery.

At one point the two men stood on the tee for 25 minutes while one of the women searched the ground a few yards down the fairway.

"Why don't you help your friend find her ball?" one of the men yelled to the second woman, who was watching her partner search.

"Oh, she's got her ball," the woman replied sweetly. "She's looking for her club."

POSITION IN LIFE

Floyd Patterson brooded for days after he was knocked out by Ingemar Johansson. Finally he went out for a walk. When he came back, he had a joke to tell.

"I walked around and nobody knew me. Then I sat down on a bench—and everyone recognized me."

ANIMAL KINGDOM

The city dweller took his young son to the state fair, where he pointed out the champion bulls, champion pigs, champion sheep, and champion chickens. Then he asked, "Any questions, son?"

"Yes, Dad, who did they have to fight to become champions?"

About the Author and Artist

Ever since Herman L. Masin launched his regular humor column in *Scholastic Coach* magazine in 1942, he has become the heavyweight champion of the sports anecdote collectors. This book is his eighth anthology of humorous anecdotes. He is also the author of three how-to-play texts, 55 booklets, numerous magazine articles, and a weekly sports column for Scholastic Magazines. A basketball analyst on television, a technical advisor on sports films, a consultant to magazines, and a record reviewer specializing in folk music and traditional jazz. On the seventh day, he rests.

Kevin Callahan has been a freelance illustrator of books, advertisements, and commercials since 1968. A former art director for major New York advertising agencies, he has received awards from the Society of Illustrators, the Society of Publication Designers, and the Advertising Club of N.Y. He lives in Norwalk, Conn.